STEEL CITY

An Illustrated History of Sheffield's Industry

Ian D. Rotherham

AMBERLEY

First published 2018

Amberley Publishing
The Hill, Stroud
Gloucestershire, GL5 4EP

www.amberleybooks.com

British Library Cataloguing in Publication Data.
A catalogue record for this book is available from the British Library.

ISBN 978 1 4456 6918 2 (print)
ISBN 978 1 4456 6919 9 (ebook)

Origination by Amberley Publishing.
Printed in Great Britain.

Contents

Preamble

Sheffield has an enviable reputation for manufacturing quality, and as a global 'steel city'; the home of major innovations in steel manufacture and processing. Furthermore, 'Sheffield plate' and Sheffield cutlery have been marques of the best in the world. By the 1200s, Sheffield had not only a 'smith' but significantly a 'cutler', and by the 1300s there were forty smiths, three arrowsmiths and three cutlers. King Edward III (d. 1377) possessed a Sheffield-made knife among his possessions in the Tower of London. Yet the story of Sheffield industry is much more than simply a catalogue of the rise of steel manufacturing and processing. One of the first major industries was located to the north of Sheffield at Wharncliffe Crags (Quern-cliff Crags), and the site of one of the Roman Empire's largest grindstone or quern-stone manufacturing sites. Like later and better known industrial ventures, the querns were made here because the quarried stone was the best and most suitable that could be found.

The industry developed in and around Sheffield because of a remarkable coincidence of woodland to make fuelwood, 'white coal' and charcoal, with rivers for water power, and mineral wealth to provide, for example, mineral coal, iron and ganister. Small-scale extraction and processing of metal and then coal, documented from the twelfth century, or earlier, began where opportunities arose and accessibility was a key factor. Once metal had been extracted, smelted and processed, this was then the raw material for independent mills, with smiths and other craftsmen springing up along watercourses where free hydro-power could turn the machinery necessary for the transformation of raw metal into useful goods, especially small hand-tools such as scythes and sickles. Later, as the industry grew and specialised, knife grinders and file makers also came to prominence, and again, were mostly smaller, independent or family run concerns.

By the eighteenth and nineteenth centuries, both coal extraction and steel manufacture boomed as the British Empire spread around the world, and Sheffield grew dramatically from a small provincial town to a major city. It was here that much of the pioneering development of the Industrial Revolution took place and Sheffield became a worldwide powerhouse for modern industrialisation. Drawn by the economic power of industry, people came to the city from the local, rural hinterland, but also from further afield. Housing for rich and poor spread across the region and the landscape was transformed. This spectacular success came at a price, with both an environmental and human toll, and it was only by the mid to late twentieth century that pollution, environmental degradation and industrial diseases were recognised and, to some extent at least, addressed.

Alongside the obvious Sheffield industries, other manufacturing and service sectors grew apace: glass-making, brewing, refractory products, power generation, joinery and associated manufacturing, water supply, waste disposal and recycling, transportation, education, health and local government. These are just some of the industries that grew up around the expanding powerhouse as an economic growth-pole, and included agriculture to supply the townsfolk, woodland management and forestry, to supply wood and timber. There were also essential trades such as tanning to make leather, and industries like brickmaking and stone quarrying, including the famous 'millstone grit', were all essential for a growing manufacturing centre. The growth of industry also triggered and fed services such as retail, hospitality and health, and the administrative sectors such as legal, financial and accounting provision, sales and marketing etc., together with the emergence of arts, the theatres and sports. The story of Sheffield's industries is so much more than just of steel and coal.

The mass-production industries slipped back against global competition during the latter twentieth century, as outdated factories and outmoded production meant foreign competition, often producing inferior but cheaper products, closed Sheffield factories down. However, the specialist skills developed in the city over centuries, supported by two major universities, now mean that the city boasts leading-edge manufacturing of specialist steel and high-tech engineering products. Sheffield therefore entered a new millennium poised to maintain its reputation for industrial and manufacturing excellence.

Niagara Weir on the River Don at Wadsley Bridge near Hillsborough in 1909.

Rivelin Bridge, Rivelin Valley, in 1904.

Rivelin waterfall near an old watermill in the early 1900s.

River Don at Niagara Falls, Hillsborough, Sheffield, in probably the 1930s.

Sheffield at work in the 1920s.

Sheffield 'soots' you, 1911.

View of Sheffield from the rural Don Valley in the 1820s.

Above: White Rails, River Don, Sheffield, by Hayward Young in the early 1900s.

Left: Work-a-day Sheffield by Hayward Young, showing the River Don and Blonk Bridge in the early 1900s – the river by then grossly polluted by the growing industrial development.

Introduction

Industry in the Sheffield area arose and evolved as it did for a number of complex reasons. However, the key is essentially location, location, location... The village, then town, now city, is located at the confluence of several rivers and seven hills as described by George Orwell in *The Road to Wigan Pier* (1936): 'The town is very hilly (said to be built on seven hills, like Rome) and everywhere streets of mean little houses blackened by smoke run up at sharp angles, paved with cobbles which are purposely set unevenly to give horses etc., a grip.' Orwell was slightly misinformed since there are the main rivers: Sheaf, Don, Porter Brook, Rivelin, and Loxley. These entail numerous tributaries, the more urban of which are today locked into fixed banks or, worse still, hidden under concrete and tarmac, but which include the Meersbrook, the Blackburn Brook, the Limb Brook, Totley Brook, and Carr Brook, for example. However, the point is made that Sheffield centre grew around the confluence of the Porter, Sheaf and Don, and at a main crossing point of the greater river, the Don, in medieval times. Historically, Sheffield was also a border settlement between the great northern upland zone and the southern lowlands; and arguably remains so today! Development along the rivers in the foothills of the great chain of the Pennines (the spine of England) meant reliable and abundant water for manufacturing processes, and critically for power. At this point the very hills of Sheffield come into play since it was the geology that was vital for local industry, providing ironstone, quarry-stone for building, mineral coal, fine-grained, hard ganister for refractory linings and of course the coarser sandstone and gritstone for making grindstones. Finally, the geology and topography of Sheffield encouraged the growth and ultimately the conservation and management of woods to produce essential timber for construction and wood for fuel, charcoal and things such as handles for small metal tools and for pit-props. The coincidence of these factors in this one place was ultimately the key to the emergence of industrial Sheffield; remarkable really when we consider that this small settlement was relatively isolated in terms of easy transport and trading. Well away from the coast and on rivers unsuited to navigation, before canals, railways and then metalled roads, Sheffield might easily have been a commercial backwater.

Sheffield is the main city within the greater South Yorkshire region. With a long history of industrial development, mineral coal mining and steel manufacture, this was a world leader of the Industrial Revolution. However, during the 1970s, there began a dramatic downturn in the industrial economy, leaving a legacy of environmental pollution and land degradation, and a history of chronic ill health associated with industrial disease. A period of rapid transformation, of major political unrest and industrial strike action, and the closure of many traditional industries and their factories, followed.

Unemployment grew to around 20 per cent of the working population and both social and environmental problems increased. In response to this challenging situation, regional stakeholders – business, politicians, workers and the community – began to adapt to the new circumstances.

A long process of environmental recovery and restoration began in order to both recycle derelict lands to make them available for new development and, importantly, to change the poor perceptions of the region. Critical steps with both planning and management interventions were undertaken to facilitate the processes of recovery. In particular, there was a sequential process of 'cleaning and greening' and re-branding, of re-structuring critical infrastructure and then, through major intervention, the kick-starting of a new economy through sports mega events, leisure retail and entertainments.

Urbanisation and industry transformed landscapes and environments across the city region, both directly and indirectly. At the heart of the process was the historic River Don, which provided a focus for the first coordinated actions to renew and regenerate the Don Valley. In 2007, the consequences of centuries of human impact on the watercourse and its wider catchment became obvious as the region was subjected to the worst floods ever recorded here. However, today the river is ecologically renewed. It has re-emerged as a vital living artery for the city, linking people, nature and place. The evidence of the timelines of historic change is still visible today.

Sheffield and its hinterland of South Yorkshire are located in the north of the English Midlands. A major river system, the Don to the Humber, flows to the east and out to the North Sea, and the high ground of the Peak District National Park is to the west. Until the 1600s or 1700s, this was largely an ancient landscape of wetlands, rivers, moors, commons, woods and forests, and deer parks and chases. There was some localised industry linked to early metalworking, coppice woodland management and especially to waterpower from the rivers. Urban development was restricted to small riverside settlements of a few thousand people in Sheffield, Rotherham, Chesterfield, Barnsley and Doncaster. Some of these originated perhaps 1,500 years ago, in Roman times.

From the early 1600s, Sheffield grew in under 200 years from around 10,000 people to over 300,000 to become a capital of world industry covering around 300 square kilometres of varied landform. This growth centred on a series of river valleys and hills, and the area has over eighty ancient woods, extensive heather moorland and bog, together with urban relict grasslands and remarkable post-industrial sites. The rivers and valleys running from the high western ground to the lowlands act as the spokes of a wheel converging on the city centre. These provide a network of natural green corridors, allowing the persistence of semi-natural wildlife areas into the heart of the city.

Through industrialisation and urbanisation over a period of around 500 years, Sheffield and South Yorkshire changed from primarily rural to massively industrial, and then in the late twentieth century to post-industrial. The recent drivers of change have included post-industrial urban renewal with the catalysts of sport, leisure, tourism, education and environment. These have combined to transform both places and people, and the latest major driver is the development of the Advanced Manufacturing Centre in the heartland of former industry and more recent dereliction. Like a phoenix, Sheffield once more rises from the ashes.

"BEAUTIFUL SHEFFIELD"   H 1045

Above: Beautiful
Sheffield, 1920s.

Right: Eminent
Sheffield industrialist
Sir John Brown, 1800s.

Above: Inside a Sheffield works at Abbeydale Industrial Hamlet. (Ian Rotherham)

Left: Local industrialist Mr George Wilson of Charles Cammell & Co. Ltd Cyclops Works, late 1800s.

Mousehole Forge, Malin Bridge, in the 1970s.

Rivelin Valley in about 1906.

Sheffield from the south in the late 1800s.

Sheffield strikers in the 1920s.

Somewhere the sun is shining – but not in Sheffield.

THE BRIGHTNESS OF BRIGHTSIDE. 2468.

Above: The bright side of Brightside, 1950s.

Right: The Canal Basin today. (Ian Rotherham)

The distress in Sheffield, with soup distribution at Brightside, 1878.

The industrial Loxley Valley in the early 1900s.

The Norfolk Arms
Hotel, Manchester Road,
with autobus in the
early 1900s.

The Old Forge, Whiteley
Woods, Sheffield, in the
early 1900s.

Upper Cut Mill, Rivelin,
in about 1914.

The First Industries

A world leader of the Industrial Revolution, Sheffield has a long history of industrial development, mineral coal mining and steel manufacture. However, during the 1970s, there began a dramatic downturn in the industrial economy, leaving a legacy of environmental pollution and land degradation, and a history of chronic ill health associated with industrial disease. Decline was followed by a period of rapid transformation, of major political unrest and industrial strike action, and the closure of many traditional industries and their factories. Unemployment grew to around 20 per cent of the working population and both social and environmental problems grew. In response to this challenging situation regional stakeholders began to adapt to the new circumstances. A long process of environmental recovery and restoration began in order to both recycle derelict lands to make them available for new development and to change the poor perceptions of the region. Some critical steps were taken to facilitate the processes of recovery and these are described later. The broad situation was described in my book, *Lost Sheffield in Colour*, and this neatly summarises Sheffield in the early to mid- twentieth century:

> Sheffield is the fourth largest city in England, and despite its history of steel, iron, coal and manufacturing, boasts more ancient woodlands than any other industrial centre in Western Europe. It is a remarkable place with unique heritage and deep-seated contradictions in its character, its people and its heritage. Described by George Orwell in the *Road to Wigan Pier*, as the dirtiest, smelliest, ugliest city in the world, its name became a by-word for clean air.

> *... But even Wigan is beautiful compared with Sheffield. Sheffield, I suppose, could justly claim to be called the ugliest town in the Old World; its inhabitants. Who want it to be pre-eminent in everything, very likely do make that claim for it ... And the stench! If at rare moments you stop smelling sulphur it is because you have begun smelling gas. Even the shallow river that runs through the town is usually bright yellow with some chemical or other. Once, I halted in the street and counted the factory chimneys I could see; there were thirty-three of them, but there would have been far more if the air had not been obscured by smoke.*

> George Orwell, 1937

Orwell goes on to point out that while there is no inherent reason why industry should be dirty and ugly, 'Northerners' have become used to and tolerant of these conditions. Today, as Melvyn Jones points out, Sheffield is the most wooded industrial city in Western Europe. Poet

Laureate John Betjeman praised the western suburbs of Sheffield as some of the greenest and prettiest in England. This is a part of the mixed up personality of Sheffield. The city, which led the Industrial Revolution, also gave rise to campaigns for access to the countryside and ultimately both National Parks and Green Belts. Sheffield was where the Industrial Revolution began in earnest and became the biggest steel manufacturing centre in Europe. The city's high-quality steels and fine cutlery were and still are, famous across the world. Today there are two large universities and at Meadowhall the biggest shopping centre in Europe, yet there is so much more to its history and its heritage. As a border town between north and south, from the Romans onwards, this region was significant in national politics and power. The great Saxon Kingdom of Northumbria extended from here north to Edinburgh, and to the south was Mercia, the powerhouse of a united English kingdom. The River Don divided the north from the south, a division reinforced by great wetlands and wooded areas of higher ground. To this day, Sheffield is a border town; the south of the north rather than the north of the south, and the lowland edge of the uplands, not vice versa.

Above left: Charcoal burner's hut in Old Park Wood, near Sheffield, from Addy, 1898.

Above right: One of the great waterwheels at Abbeydale Industrial Hamlet. (Ian Rotherham)

Old Tower Wheel on the River Don in the early 1800s.

Sheffield Town Hall in the 1700s, a symbol of the town's growing status.

Right: Smelting iron in a basic early blast furnace.

Below: The memorial to George Yardley, wood-collier, Ecclesall Woods – where he burned to death in his cabin in October 1786. The memorial was erected by his drinking pals from the Rising Sun Inn, just a half mile away.

View from Bole Hills, Walkley, in the early 1900s.

Wharncliffe Crags – one of the region's first industrial sites, dating back to the Romans.

Wharncliffe Crags had grindstone manufacturing, and also ganister mines, until the 1900s but by the 1800s was also a popular 'picturesque' tourism destination. The image shows tourists in the early 1900s.

Coal Mining

In the classic account of Sheffield's history written by Mary Walton in 1948, she notes that 'Sheffield is not primarily a colliery town ... but coal and coke had been vital needs to the other local industries ever since the earl of Shrewsbury'. Indeed, the Lords of the Manor had kept a tight grip on the monopoly of coal mined in the great park. All that slowed the progress of coal mining development in the area was the problem of transportation, which made the Handsworth collieries uneconomical and made the working of the Staniforth colliery at Attercliffe problematic.

The availability of mineral coal was of importance in the region from the very earliest times of recorded 'industry', i.e. the Romans, and it is noted that they burnt coal at their station at Templeborough. By medieval times coal was more widely used but with it came problems and limitations. The nature of mineral coal means that burning in an open fireplace without a chimney was difficult and could even be dangerous – with poisoning through inhalation of carbon monoxide a serious risk and other impurities and heavy smoke most unpleasant. This meant the use of coal for domestic fires was restricted, and of course a further consideration was cost; coal was expensive and some other fuels were free for the gathering. The other main complication was occurrence of and access to coal seams. In the Sheffield area, for instance, the rock strata of the Coal Measures Series geology dip deep underground from west to east. This means that the coal outcrops at or near the surface, though often with thinner seams, are to the western side of Sheffield. It was here that the first mineral coal extraction took place with bell pits from the surface and adits or drifts into the hillside almost horizontally. The thickness and quality of coal increased as the rocks occurred through the town and then to the east towards Barnsley, Rotherham and Doncaster, but they also dipped deep underground. The latter point meant that the coal was only accessible via deep-mining and this necessitated the use of steam-powered pumps to remove excess ground water. Such pumps were only becoming available in the 1700s and into the 1800s, and so prior to that time deep-mined coal was inaccessible. By the 1720s, Thomas Newcomen was pumping water in all the region's deep mines. An early reference to coal mining in the township comes in an undated charter probably from the late 1200s, giving the monks at Beauchief Abbey the right to 'dig, raise, take and carry for their use and profit of themselves and their tenants both bond and free' sea coal in both Alfreton and Norton, the former not actually in Sheffield itself, and the latter at that time in Derbsyhire. By the 1500s, Sheffield's reputation for coal mining was growing and the Lord of the Manor, the 6th Earl of Shrewsbury, was described by Lord Burghley as 'a great collier'.

As demand for mineral coal grew in the medieval period, bell pits, drift mines (or adits) and shallow-shaft mines dotted the region on a small scale as and where coal outcropped. However, by around 200 years ago the easily worked coal had mostly gone and deeper mines with efficient pumps allowed the more easterly seams to be worked. By the 1960s, around 50,000 miners were employed at about fifty individual pits in the South Yorkshire coalfield. These were mostly in the Middle Coal Measures belt in the exposed coalfield and the shafts had originally been sunk in the mid-1800s in pursuit of the 3-metre-thick Barnsley seam. From around 1908 the shafts were bigger and deeper as the miners went after the concealed coalfield far underground. The risks were greater and the production of waste or 'overburden' was also vastly increased, resulting in the classic slag heaps that occurred across the coalfields region. By 1913, the Yorkshire coalfield employed over 270,000 people and produced over 74 million tons of coal per year.

In Sheffield itself there were several major deep-shaft mines and many lesser ones. Sites included the Birley Collieries group (closed 1940s), High Hazels Colliery (closed 1947), Handsworth (closed 1967), Nunnery Colliery (closed 1953), Rother Vale Collieries, Orgreave (closed 1981), Smithy Wood (closed 1972), Thorncliffe (closed 1954), Brookhouse (closed 1985) and Tinsley Park Collieries. Others included Handsworth and Handsworth Woodhouse (closing 1871 and 1854 respectively), Hall Park at Stannington (closed 1881), Haighenfield at Loxley (closed 1905), Hagg Stones at Worral (closed 1938), Hand Lane at Crane Moor (closed 1907), High Wincobank (closed 1902 and again 1912), Hurfield Hill at Heeley (closed 1923), Hurlfield (closed 1881) and Hutcliffe Wood at Millhouses (closed 1934). Some of these were small sites and many were short-lived; Heywood at Deepcar, for example, opened in 1873 and was abandoned in 1874. Others closed only to re-open at a later date. Nationalisation of the coal industry in 1947 had a dramatic effect on the region's mines until the closure of most sites through the Thatcher cuts in the 1980s.

An important development in coal mining technology occurred at a pit close by Arbourthorne Farm, near the manorial estate. The colliery was rented from the Duke of Norfolk by two men, Townsend and Furness, and in 1775 one of their employees, John Curr, invented a narrow-gauge cast-iron railroad with L-shaped rails. Up until this time railways and waggonways had run on wooden rails, such as one developed by Townsend and Furness to carry coals to their yard in Sheffield. Curr was headhunted by Vincent Eyre, the agent of the Earl of Surrey, Lord of Hallamshire, when he decided to take over the colliery operation himself. Curr published his drawings of his rails and the tubs or 'corves' in the *Colliery Viewer*, and the same designs were still in widespread use well into the twentieth century as the standard for underground transport. For above-ground work the Curr system was fine with horse-drawn wagons, but was unsuited to locomotive-drawn wagons, which required wrought-iron rails.

Another influence on local coal mining was the arrival of the Sheffield & Tinsley Canal in 1819, and then of the railway in 1838. Renting the collieries in the manor park from the Duke of Norfolk, the Sheffield Coal Company had enjoyed a monopoly on the local coal trade because of their proximity to the town and the difficulty of getting other sources in. One quick result of the new canal arriving was the opening of a colliery at the Tinsley end of the canal by the Earl Fitzwilliam. However, the advent of the new and cheaper transport meant that collieries from farther away could provide coal to the emerging heavy industries and could do this at a competitive price.

A major influence on the region's coal mining, almost on the scale of the Thatcher cuts, was the wartime emergency measures that triggered a spate of open-cast coaling, which carried on until the 1990s and indeed was the fate of many former deep-coal sites and their spoil heaps. Open-casting was contentious as a competitor with deep mines and mass employment, and through its sometime horrific environmental and other impacts. However, open-casting and associated restoration was also used to clean away environmental dereliction and pollution and to create new sites such as Tinley Park (airport, hotel, nature reserve and business park for example) and nearby Rother Valley Country Park.

Like many other major industries, coal mining had an associated network of supplier trades and industries, and also close connections to other, in this case energy-demanding, enterprises such as iron and steel manufacture. In the coal industry, one particular valuable but environmentally damaging association was with the coking process to produce much-needed chemical by-products, such as volatile organic compounds like oils. The collateral damage to human health and the local environment has never been fully quantified but was clearly massive. Major sites included Orgeave and others to the south along the Rother Valley and around Smithy Wood in the north-east.

The coal industry in Sheffield, and even now across the wider region, has gone, but it is interesting to note the view of the local miners recorded by H. Stanley Jevons in his classic *The Coal Trade* in 1915. He noted that the pay and conditions for Yorkshire miners were lower than those in other regions, but also that the miners' union, the Yorkshire Miners' Association, had 90,000 members. His comments on things like housing give a brief insight into the lives of the workers who 'live in dirty, ill-made, noisy streets under a murky atmosphere; and many of the cottages being built back to back there is no through ventilation and no privacy'. Jevons goes on, stating, 'The Yorkshire miner is on the whole rather a rougher type than his confrères of Durham, Scotland, or South Wales.' Furthermore, 'His recreations are less intellectual, and ... Yorkshire miners have been great devotees of cock-fighting and hare coursing ... the pit-boys are rather notorious as a wild and rough lot.'

Pit-pony at work in a coal mine in the early 1900s; they were still in use into the mid-twentieth century in places like Shire Brook Valley.

The River Don Navigation in the early 1900s became a main artery for the transport of materials in and the transport of manufactured goods or coal out.

The River Don Navigation from Hexthorpe Flatts in the early 1900s – this route linked Sheffield, Rotherham, Doncaster and potentially downstream beyond.

Men working underground at the pit in the early 1900s.

Hewing the coal underground at the pit in the early 1900s.

Iron and Steel

Iron manufacture

It is suggested that the Romans were smelting iron on a large scale associated with their Templeborough fortress just east of Sheffield's Don Valley. This would make sense since metalworking was essential for the manufacture of weapons and or armour. Furthermore, the Romans or Romano-British were certainly capable of large-scale industrial working in the area as is evidenced by the massive grindstone-manufacturing works at Wharncliffe, above Stocksbridge. By medieval times, the monks of Kirkstead Abbey had the rights to iron smelting and mining around Kimberworth and Kirkstead Abbey Grange at Thorpe Hesley was connected to their operations. Such early industry was also happening in the heart of medieval Sheffield, which was still just a small town, and can be seen in things such as a grant in 1268 of a third part of money coming from smithies in 'Schefeuld' and 'Halumpshire'. This was to the Dowager Lady Furnival relating to wood from the Park and quarries in 'Riveling', and a century later the Lord of Sheffield manor was still receiving income from the same sites. By around 1379, the Poll Tax records testify to twenty-two smiths and five cutlers operating in the area.

Ironstone occurs widely in the coal measures geology of the Sheffield area and a particularly notable seam is the Tankersley ironstone. Mining from early times up to the 1800s was by shallow bell pits sunk vertically into the ground and examples of these can be seen on Tankersley Golf Course from the M1 motorway. There were deeper shafts suck as well, but by the 1880s, local ironstone had become uneconomic in the face of larger-scale extraction in places like Scunthorpe and mining ceased. Superficially at least, ironstone bell pits and coal bell pits look rather similar, and in many places both must have been in use.

In the late 1500s, charcoal-fuelled blast furnaces arrived in the Sheffield area and displaced the more primitive bloomeries. By the mid-1700s, there were blast furnaces across the region with ironstone bell pits around them and coppice woods providing the necessary charcoal. Close by the furnace would be a water-powered forge on the nearby river, such as at Wortley, Wadsley, and Attercliffe on the River Don. The processes changed again with the successful use of mineral coke for iron smelting by Abraham Darby in 1709, loosening the need for wood-based charcoal. The new coke-fuelled blast furnaces were soon in place at locations such as Thorncliffe, Parkgate and further afield, like Elsecar. These furnaces produced pig iron that led to a burgeoning cast-iron and wrought-iron industry in the region; something which differed from the light steel trades of Sheffield itself. These various initiatives allowed Sheffield and its wider region to benefit from the other industrial and domestic innovations of the time – becoming a provider of heavy engineering for the railways, for military needs, for gas appliances and fittings, for fire grates and hearths, and for the ornamental cast iron trade.

Sheffield Steel

Sheffield's rise to fame as an industrial centre was built originally on its small tools and its cutlery manufacture. Locally accessible supplies of charcoal and wood were important in the developing industries, as was sandstone suitable for grindstone manufacture, and, above all, water power. Steel-based manufacturers sprang up along all the main watercourses. By around 1660 there were already over fifty water-powered sites in the area; by 1740, around ninety, and by 1770 Sheffield had 161 water-powered workshops. These often modestly sized factories were making steel and manufacturing sharp-edge tools. From the mid-1700s, the use of charcoal was being displaced by the newly refined use of mineral coke, and this was helped by the application of Huntsman's crucible process (*see below*). Finally, by the late 1700s and early 1800s, water power was being replaced by steam engines. However, water power was still used in some factories right up until the 1950s; after all, water power was free, if unreliable, whereas steam power cost money! The shift from water power meant workshops could be located at distances farther away from the rivers, and closer to the sites of coke manufacture. While some larger factories began to develop, the typical manufacturing unit was still the smaller workshop.

The townsfolk produced iron but imported steel when they needed it. Indeed, this situation carried on until around 1750, with steel being brought in from Europe, and then from Newcastle by the early 1700s. However, from around 1750 to the early 1800s, steelmaking was revolutionised by what became known as 'the Sheffield methods' – i.e. the manufacture of 'blister steel' in cementation furnaces and the melting of the steel in crucibles. The process was invented by Lincolnshire-born Benjamin Huntsman and produced 'cast steel' as small ingots.

Huntsman was an interesting character who had a critical influence on Sheffield, and indeed world, history. He was the fourth child of William and Mary Huntsman, a Quaker couple who farmed at Epworth in North Lincolnshire. Benjamin began work as a clock, lock and tool maker in Doncaster and soon his reputation grew. Somehow this allowed him to practice experimental surgery, perhaps linked to his skill in manipulating small and sharp metal tools; clearly an entrepreneur, he also set up as a consultant oculist.

However, Huntsman's great breakthrough was with his experiments in steelmaking and this was initially in Doncaster rather than Sheffield. In 1740 he moved to Handsworth, then on the outskirts of the expanding town of Sheffield. Through painstaking experimentation Huntsman was eventually able to produce a good cast steel manufactured in clay pot crucibles. Each crucible held around 34 lb of 'blistered steel'. After adding a 'flux' (such as limestone as a cleansing or purifying agent) to the mix, they were covered and heated with mineral coke for a further three hours, after which the molten steel was poured into moulds. The crucibles could then be reused.

Despite being so close to what was to be a revolutionary discovery, local cutlery manufacturers were reluctant to adopt new materials and refused to buy Huntsman's cast steel. Since it was harder than the imported German steel they were used to working, it was more difficult to use. Indeed, for some years Huntsman had to export his entire production to France, but this led to serious problems for local industry. Using Huntsman's superior steel, the French cutlery manufacturers began to have great success, and imports of their products became a threat to the Sheffield cutlery makers. The latter were so alarmed that they even tried (unsuccessfully) to get the British government to ban the export of Huntsman's steel. Eventually, having realised the superior product, the local firms caved in and adopted his material. Despite this breakthrough Huntsman still faced problems, since for some reason he had not patented his unique process. Perhaps through intrigue, his secret was discovered by a Sheffield iron-founder named Walker. According to legend, he was supposed to have got into Huntsman's works one night while disguised as a starving beggar who asked to sleep by the fire. The consequence was that other steelmakers were able to cut in on the new process.

By 1770 Benjamin Huntsman had relocated his business to Worksop Road in Attercliffe, and there he prospered until his death in 1776. His body was interred in a commemorative tomb in Hilltop Cemetery, on Attercliffe Common, and the works were taken over by his son, William Huntsman (1733–1809).

Largely based on the two methods developed by Huntsman, Sheffield steel prospered throughout the period from around 1800 to about 1865. Consequently, production capacity grew from around 3,000 tons per annum to upwards of 100,000 tons, with, of course, an associated increase in gross pollution of land, water and air, and a rapid rise in the human population from about 10,000 in 1700 to over 400,000 by the early 1900s. From the 1860s, other methods began to be adopted for mass steel manufacture – notably the Bessemer and open-hearth processes. These grew in parallel with older 'Sheffield methods', which probably peaked in terms of output around 1873 at about 120,000 tons per annum. The old and new approaches continued together.

However, a further transformation was to occur, with Sheffield developing from around the 1880s as a centre for the development and manufacture of 'special steels'; and it is perhaps this innovation that has carried the city forward even to the present day. With open-hearth processes generating bulk steel, there were factories to make heavy items for ordnance and for shipbuilding, and for other heavy engineering requirements. One trigger for the changes to come was the invention in 1879 by Gilchrist Thomas of the basic steelmaking process, which helped steel manufacturing to grow around the world and bulk steel to move from Sheffield to the greater ore fields. With increased steel production, however, came a growth in demand for hard tools to machine it, and Sheffield industry was kept busy making producing saws and files and turning machinery.

As carbon steel morphed into the production of alloy steel and today's special steels, Sheffield's industry grew into the new challenges.

The rolling of armour plate in Sheffield at the Atlas Steelworks in the late 1800s.

A 4,000-ton press at Firth Brown Limited in the 1960s.

Queen Victoria witnessing the rolling of armour plate at Messrs Cammell's works in 1897.

Abbeydale Industrial Hamlet in the 1970s.

Barrel for a huge naval gun – turning a steel jacket at Vickers' works in 1905.

Casting a monster anvil block at the Midland Works.

Casting railway tyres in 1875.

Coiling springs at Cammell Laird during the First World War.

Above: Drawing armour plate from the furnace, 1875.

Left: Forging a gun-tube under a 6,000-ton press at Vickers' River Don Works in 1905.

Large plate rolling
mill, Davy Brothers,
Sheffield, 1921.

Large plate rolling
mill, Davy Brothers,
Sheffield, 1921.

Rolling a large armour
plate ingot at the River
Don Works, with men
applying beesoms
to the hot metal.
(*The Sphere*, 1905)

Sheffield steel melters in 1914.

Crucibles for steelmaking at Abbeydale Industrial Hamlet. (Ian Rotherham)

Right: Steam-hammer at the forging press of the Atlas Steel & Iron Works in the early 1900s.

Below: Thorncliffe Works, Sheffield, 1909.

THORNCLIFFE WORKS.

Munitions workers at
Cammell Laird during
the First World War.

Making armour plate
at Cammell Laird,
First World War, with
a 12,000-ton press.

Making laminated
railway springs at
Cammell Laird during
the First World War.

Making Bessemer
steel in the
early 1900s.

Forging bloom for
axles at Cammell
Laird in the
early 1900s.

Edgar Allen & Co.

Dinner hour meeting of the
Open Air Mission at the
East Hecla Steel Works in
the 1920s.

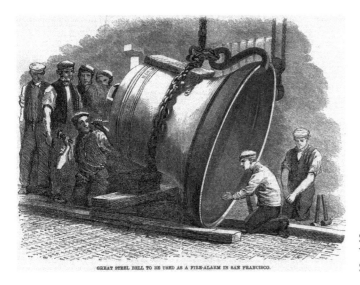

GREAT STEEL BELL TO BE USED AS A FIRE-ALARM IN SAN FRANCISCO.

Steel cast bell at Naylor,
Vickers & Co., Millsands,
Sheffield, in 1860.

River Don Steam Engine
built by Davy Brothers in
1905 to power the Charles
Cammell armour plate
rolling mill.

Steel melting
shop, teeming
molten steel in the
early 1900s.

Making steel
for pens at
Jessop's Works,
late 1800s.

Stocksbridge
Steel Works,
around 1900.

Left: The King and Queen in 1905, watching the rolling of armour plate in Sheffield at Vickers' gun factory.

Below: Turning heavy shells on lathes at Cammell Laird during the First World War.

A First World War munitions worker.

John Brown's Atlas Steel & Spring Works around 1875. Note the Midland Railway line in the background.

Left: Walker & Hall Electro Works, Howard Street, mid-1800s.

Below: William Turner & Son cast steel.

WILLIAM TURNER & SON,

MANUFACTURERS OF

WARRANTED CAST STEEL,

For TURNING TOOLS, TAPS, DIES, BURRS, CHISELS, PUNCHES, COLD SATES, SHEAR BLADES, Etc. Etc.

WARRANTED DOUBLE SHEAR STEEL FOR WELDING, SPRING AND BLISTER STEEL.

Warranted CAST STEEL FILES,

FOR ENGINEERS' AND SMITHS' USE.

ROLL TURNING TOOLS.

Swaged Circular Saws for Cutting Iron.

SOLID CAST STEEL ENGINEERS' HAND & SLEDGE HAMMERS, & ENGINEERS' TOOLS.

CALEDONIA STEEL AND FILE WORKS,

SHEFFIELD.

Cutlery, Plate and Small Tools

Sheffield makers of small tools received a publicity boost courtesy of Geoffrey Chaucer in the fourteen century with his reference to 'The Sheffield Thwitel' (or Thwytel):

> Ther was no man, for peril, dorste hym touche. A Sheffeld thwitel baar he in his hose. Round was his face, and camus was his nose.

> Geoffrey Chaucer, 'The Reeve's Tale',
> *Canterbury Tales. c.* 1388

This also confirms the well-established name of 'Sheffield' in such manufacture at that early date. Indeed, by the early 1500s, Sheffield was alongside Birmingham in becoming known as a centre for such works and competition from places like York, Beverley and Chester, for example, had tailed off.

One of Sheffield's advantages was its abundant water power, which was essential for heavy industry in the pre-petro-chemical age. Much of the earliest use of water power was in the lower-lying rivers such as at Lescar, the Sheaf, and often to the east or north of the main town centre – for example, Ecclesfield, Wisewood, Holbrook, Wadsley Bridge, Shire Brook and Little Sheffield. Mills then sprang up all along the Porter, the Sheaf, the Loxley, the Don and the associated tributaries. By 1637, the Lordship of Sheffield Manor was leasing over twenty-eight 'cutler wheels'. Other owners had similar enterprises at Ecclesfield and both Eckington in Derbyshire and Norton (formerly in Derbyshire).

Sheffield Plate – The Poor Man's Silverware

Sheffield's metalworkers were mostly independent 'little mesters', working in a small workshop with living quarters above, and often for a number of larger firms. The town was noted for high-quality metal goods but in the 1700s was still relatively small and relatively poor. The invention by Thomas Boulsover of 'Sheffield plate' in the 1700s did much to change all this. He realised that by fusing a thin layer of silver onto a thicker sheet of copper by heating, the composite metal could be worked much as pure silver to produce good-quality tableware and other ornaments, but at a fraction of the usual price. In simple terms this was imitation silverware, which allowed the aspirational middle classes to indulge in fancy items that previously they could not afford. Boulsover himself did not fully exploit the potential of his discovery and left that to others such as Joseph Hancock. The latter switched from silversmithing to set up the Old Park Rolling Mills in around 1770, which produced sheets of fused metal for use as Sheffield plate. John Read had a business recycling and extracting silver from scrap metal to go back into the trade. His Sheffield Smelting Company later became Engelhard Industries.

Boulsover was not the only innovator in Sheffield metalworking as craftsmen sought to produce cheaper goods to match the luxury-end silverware. One of the traditional materials was pewter, a substance that varied in constituents quite markedly. Pewter is a malleable metal alloy and was traditionally composed of 85 per cent to 99 per cent tin mixed with copper, antimony, bismuth and sometimes lead. The latter could be a significant part of the alloy but we now know it carries serious health issues for the consumer and is therefore less common today. Lead-rich pewter, more common in the lower grades, which have a bluish tint, was heavier and darker than the lighter alloys. Silver might also be added, while copper and antimony were used as hardeners. Pewter has a low melting point, from 170 degrees Celsius to 230 degrees, varying with the mix. Following on from Boulsover's discovery, James Vickers invented 'Britannia metal' as an alloy of tin, copper and antimony, which had similar properties to pewter but could be polished to a silver-like finish – the 'poor man's silver'. By the late 1800s numerous firms were set up to exploit these processes and markets; some, like James Dixon's Cornish Works, established in 1828, were quite large factories. However, by the 1840s, Sheffield plate was becoming obsolete as the process of electroplating was being developed by Elkington & Co. in Birmingham and, following them, Walker & Hall in Sheffield.

SHEFFIELD

Steel Works and Cutlery, and Electro Plate Factories.

POPULATION, 511,740.

A celebration of Sheffield, its population and its industry.

Cutlers at work in Sheffield in 1914.

Sheffield saw-smiths at work in the early 1900s.

Sheffield's famous Buffer Girls, 1905.

Sheffield's famous Buffer Girls at Cammell Laird in the early 1900s.

Right: Sheffield knife grinders in the early 1900s.

Below: Hull of the Fork-Grinders, *the Sheffield Steel Manufacturers*, 1866.

Scythe grinding in the 1800s.

Saw grinding in the 1800s.

Old-style grinding wheel in Endcliffe Wood in the 1800s.

Above: File-cutting in the 1800s.

Right: An old grinding wheel in the Rivelin Valley, early 1900s.

Rivelin Valley millpond, early 1900s.

Upper Cut Wheel at Rivelin, early 1900s.

Shepherd Wheel at Endcliffe, 1970s.

Interior of a grinding wheel, 1980s.

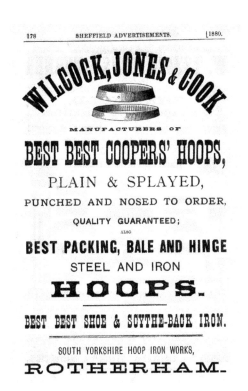

Above left: Hoop maker, 1800s.

Above right: Advertisement for Tyzack & Turner, late 1800s.

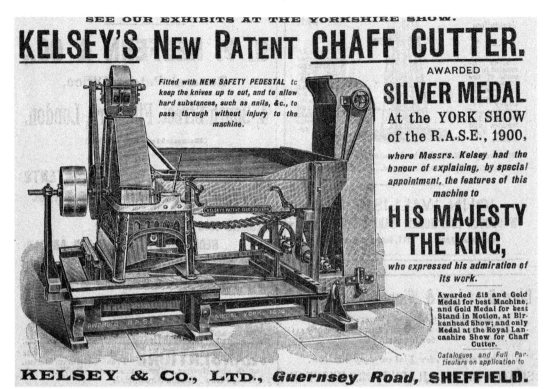

SEE OUR EXHIBITS AT THE YORKSHIRE SHOW.

KELSEY'S NEW PATENT CHAFF CUTTER.

Fitted with NEW SAFETY PEDESTAL to keep the knives up to cut, and to allow hard substances, such as nails, &c., to pass through without injury to the machine.

AWARDED

SILVER MEDAL

At the YORK SHOW of the R.A.S.E., 1900,

where Messrs. Kelsey had the honour of explaining, by special appointment, the features of this machine to

HIS MAJESTY THE KING,

who expressed his admiration of its work.

Awarded £15 and Gold Medal for best Machine, and Gold Medal for best Stand in Motion, at Birkenhead Show; and only Medal at the Royal Lancashire Show for Chaff Cutter.

Catalogues and Full Particulars on application to

KELSEY & CO., LTD., *Guernsey Road,* **SHEFFIELD.**

YEAR KNIFE
MADE IN 1822: CONTAINED 1822 BLADES, EACH BLADE WILL OPEN AND SHUT.
JOSEPH RODGERS & SONS, LTD.
SHEFFIELD.
TRADE ✸✦ MARK

Above: Kelsey's New Patent Chaff Cutter, late 1800s.

Left: The Year Knife as displayed at Weston Park Museum, made in 1822 and containing 1,822 blades.

Rivelin Valley mill in the
early 1900s.

Buffing electro-plate at
Martin, Hall & Co.'s works in
the 1800s.

Waterwheel and mill in the
Rivelin Valley, early 1900s.

Ganister, Stone and Millstone

True Grit

The importance of coal mining has already been discussed, and while that is one of the most obvious sources of the region's mineral wealth, it is by no means the only one. The geology of the region produced millstone grit for grinding stones, ganister for refractory linings, clay for brickmaking and, of course, building stone of various grades for diverse uses. Extraction sites could be massive open-cast quarries or small, very localised 'stone-getting pits'. All the Sheffield valleys are dotted with former quarry sites, and walk through any of our ancient woods and you will find many amorphous pits used to extract building stone, often for local drystone walls and the like. As my friend geologist Frank Spode said, 'You can only take the rock or the mineral where it occurs.' So for Sheffield's early industry, lead, for example, was imported from the nearby White Peak of Derbyshire; with the exception of a single small extraction site at Brightholmlee at the end of the Ewden Valley, Sheffield had no native lead sites. For building, the soft magnesian limestones were imported from quarries to the east of the town.

The local rocks are layers of the Coal Measures Series, with coal (obviously), sandstones of varying grades (from very coarse and pebbly to very fine), soft shales and mudstones or clays. These rocks shaped local topography and land use, but also offered up mineral wealth. The sandstones, being aquifers, also had important roles in the water supply. In some of the lower-lying areas east and south of the town centre, the geology has also produced occasional sources of sands, gravels and alluvial clays.

The two major uses of stone were firstly for building and secondly for the refractory linings as Sheffield's industries expanded. Up to the 1600s, most buildings (other than churches and great houses or castles) would have been largely constructed of timber and other locally sourced materials. From the 1700s onwards, stone buildings, along with brick, became more commonplace. In terms of building, the sources and grades of rock used varied with the prestige of the user. A poorer local person would make do with whatever was near at hand and available. For prestigious buildings, private houses or public places, more expensive and better grade materials would be sought. The methods of constructing also varied with time and place, giving rise to typical 'vernacular' styles of buildings. Some of the oldest sandstones in the Lower Coal Measures Series include the relatively coarse-grained Crawshaw Sandstone, which outcrops only along the southern border of Yorkshire, through West Sheffield and into Derbyshire. This stone was quarried locally and used for construction as the prosperous western suburbs of

Sheffield expanded. A thicker sandstone was the Greenmoor Rock (quarried and used at sites like Greno Wood and Brincliffe), along with Grenoside Rock. 'Millstone Grit' is a catchall description covering a range of coarse sandstones ('grits') laid down in the delta of an immense river that flowed from high ground to the east of the region. The land here was below sea level and each tide or flood dumped sand and other sediments onto the sea floor to eventually form the rocks we see today. 'Rivelin Grit' and 'Chatsworth Grit' were formed as uniform rocks without lines of weakness and have been very important for building and for the manufacture of grindstones. For a stonemason, rocks that are free from lines of weakness are good to use since they can be worked in any direction. These outcrops were used over many centuries, and indeed back to Romano-British times, to make querns and millstones for grinding corns, and then, later, to make huge grindstones for milling and for toolmaking.

Vernacular building styles depend on geology and related factors and give a location its sense of place. This region had a long tradition of construction in 'rubble' and in 'ashlar blocks', the former being angular rocks laid either courses (in layers) or uncoursed. Sometimes these were set in a more ordered herringbone fashion. Ashlar blocks were precisely worked blocks of stone, which were square, oblong or curved. By their nature the latter were costly and therefore prestigious, but by the late 1700s, the finer buildings were of this construction and even the smaller gatehouse cottages of the grand estates were done this way.

The millstone industry was once a major economic process in the western region, and many of the moorland slopes are scattered with abandoned cut and part-cut stones, and criss-crossed with deep trackways, along which the grindstones were manoeuvred and rolled out and away to markets in the UK and across Europe. This was a big industry through the 1700s and 1800s, until changing technologies and cheap imports took away the markets. Today, the grindstones are the symbol of the Peak District National Park.

Refractory Stone

At one time Sheffield was one of the main centres for the production of refractory materials in Great Britain, the early industry being based on locally mined or quarried 'fireclay' (including the famous 'pot clays' used to make the crucibles in the crucible steel process) or 'ganister'. Ganister, a fine-grained hard siliceous rock, was employed to make linings for crucible furnaces and forge furnaces, and then as a liner for acid Bessemer converters. In about 1858, based in Oughtibridge, silica bricks began to be made from locally sourced ganister and the area was soon the main producer of silica bricks in Britain. Another nearby geological outcrop to become important in steel manufacture was the magnesian limestone from the areas immediately east of Sheffield. With the advent of the basic Bessemer and basic open-hearth furnaces in the 1880s, this limestone was the main source of dolomite for the 'basic' part of the process. By the 1940s, the Loxley Valley area specialised in producing fireclays for casting-pit refractories, while silica bricks for the steel and carbonising industries were made at Oughtibridge, Deepcar, Totley and Millhouses. However, by the 1960s, the easier sources had been worked out and the high-grade raw material was being imported from elsewhere.

A millstone and the symbol of the Peak District National Park, 1970.

Bell Hagg Quarry, Crosspool, in the early 1900s.

Right: Millstones used as steps at Shepherd's Wheel in the Porter Valley. (Ian Rotherham)

Below: Millstone used at Shepherd's Wheel in the Porter Valley. (Ian Rotherham)

Above: Various grindstones stacked at Abbeydale Industrial Hamlet. (Ian Rotherham)

Left: Refactory products by Marshalls at Storrs Bridge in the 1930s.

Typical sandstone walling.
(Chris Percy)

Geologist Dr Frank Spode
inspecting a geological
quarry outcrop. (Chris Percy)

A geological quarry outcrop.
(Chris Percy)

Water, Forestry and Farming

Water Supply

A famous saying in Sheffield is the quote referring to the Sheffield Wicker, '*Dahn t'Wicker where t'watter runs o'er t'weir*', and this perhaps reflects the significance to Sheffield of the River Don, the Wicker by the old castle and particularly the ancient industrial weirs. The latter are some of the oldest built structures in the city. The river here is spanned by Lady's Bridge, one of the oldest bridges in the area, but to see the medieval bridge you have to get down to the riverside to peer underneath the modern and early industrial structures. The weir at Lady's Bridge is one of the most familiar to most Sheffielders, though there are other and bigger ones, such as Niagara Weir on the River Don at Wadsley Bridge near Hillsborough. The weirs are evidence of the historical importance of water supply and water power to local industry. Building a weir across a river was needed both to divert flow into a pond or dam, and to raise a head of water to power a water wheel. The wheel could then transfer energy and power from the water via a series of belts, gears, beams and wheels to turn the various machines needed for local industry. This might be for tasks such as grinding corn, fulling of cloth, crushing and grinding mineral ores to extract metals, and the grinding of metal implements (from things like arrowheads, spears and swords to sickles, scythes, adzes, hoes, spades and forks). There were also the specialist tools to be used by woodworkers, stonemasons, carpenters, shipwrights and others. Other uses included the powering of paper mills, and in Sheffield the great rolling mills for, initially, the rolling of copper and silver as Sheffield plate, and then later on for armour plate. The point here, however, is that water and its energy were hugely important to all of these.

As Sheffield grew from a parochial craft-industry centre to a major industrial powerhouse, harnessing the water supply became increasingly important – for the industry itself, but also for the burgeoning urban population. By the 1600s, there was a move from the small 'on-line' millponds for industry to major water supply reservoirs, the first being Barker's Pool in the town centre in 1631. Then, in 1713, the Lord of the Manor granted consent to lay pipes along highways to carry water from springs near White House in Hillsborough, and in 1737 there followed a reservoir near this same location, close by the site of the later Sheffield Barracks. By 1782, permission had been given for the construction of reservoirs at Crookesmoor, and over the period from 1785 to 1829, five individual reservoirs were built there; the last ones, Godfrey Dam and Old Dam (4 acres with a capacity of 21 million gallons of water), were still in use up to the 1950s. Godfrey is now the Sheffield University hard-surface football pitches and Old Dam is still in Crookes Valley Park.

By 1830, the Sheffield Waterworks Company became incorporated by an Act of Parliament, with capital of £100,000 and paying £41,802 to the former owners of the relevant property. This same Act empowered the company to build two major storage reservoirs at Redmires on the edge of high moorlands to the west of Sheffield and the Hadfield Reservoir at Crookes (5 acres with a capacity of 21 million gallons), which was built in 1833 and was finally covered over in 1951, and which remained in service for many decades but as a covered tank. The company were also empowered to construct a major above-ground conduit 4.5 miles long from Redmires into Sheffield at Crookes, completed in 1833. This latter structure can still be followed around Lodge Moor, but ceased to function in 1909 because of leakage and risk of pollution.

The Redmires Reservoirs were on a scale previously unknown. The Redmires Impounding Reservoir (taking water from Wyming Brook), completed in 1836, is now the middle of the three reservoirs at Redmires. When completed it had a capacity of 188 million gallons and a depth of 36 feet.

The reservoir built at Crookes was originally called 'Pisgah Dam' after Mount Pisgah in the Holy Land. However, the panoramic view across smoky Sheffield was somewhat less salubrious than a vision of the Promised Land. The name was altered to 'Hadfield Reservoir', probably after Robert Hadfield of Hadfield's Steel and Master Cutler in 1899. The open Hadfield Reservoir was in service up to 1945 when it was replaced in 1950 by the smaller (6 million-gallon) concrete-covered service reservoir. The remainder of the old dam was then in-filled and turned firstly into a sports ground for cricket, football and tennis (Sheffield Waterworks Sports Club) and more recently into housing. The covered reservoir is still used to supply south-east Sheffield with drinking water from Rivelin Water Treatment Works.

A further Act of Parliament in 1845 empowered the company to build the third Redmires Reservoir, and by 1854, with all three reservoirs, the average daily yield of water delivered to Sheffield was around 3.5 million gallons. Interestingly, the overall capacity here was much greater than the potential supply from the Wyming Brook and the surrounding ground. With continuing growth in demand, expanding industry and an increasing human population, the search was on for additional supplies and suitable reservoir sites. Parliament granted permission to construct Dam Flask, Strines, Agden and Dale Dyke, all in the Loxley Valley and associated tributaries. However, in 1864 catastrophe struck with the storm-induced collapse of the Dale Dyke Reservoir, with the loss of 244 lives and a cost in damages to the company of £373,000. This was the worst peacetime disaster of its sort in British history. Following the incorporation of the Borough in 1844, the Town Council was in almost constant dispute with Waterworks Company, finally acquiring control in 1888. There had been ongoing problems with intermittent water supply to the town, and indeed the company was under no obligation to provide such until the law changed in 1870. In 1864, for example, the year of the Dale Dyke disaster, water supply to Sheffield during a drought period had been limited to four hours per day on alternative days only; and a similar situation arose in 1870. The consequences for local communities and businesses can only be imagined. Furthermore, in order to meet the claims against them, the company successfully lobbied to be allowed to raise the water charges by 25 per cent over a twenty-five-year period. For the Town Council this situation was outrageous and they attempted, unsuccessfully, to take control of the Waterworks Company.

However, research after the Corporation's takeover showed that daily consumption in 1869 was running at around 40 gallons per head, but with the modernisation of fittings and improved efficiencies it was reduced to 13 gallons per person per day in 1890. Legal costs for disputes between the two bodies mounted and the Town Council ultimately developed a significant debt as a consequence, with the Town Clerk personally out of pocket to the tune of £2,000, which at the time was a considerable sum. The ultimate cost to the Council of buying out the company was £2,092,014 6s 11d and by this time the holdings included the three Redmires Reservoirs, Rivelin Upper and Lower Reservoirs, and the Loxley Valley chain of dams, including the rebuilt Dale Dyke. There were also the smaller service reservoirs at Crookes, the Redmires and Crookes conduits, the Ughill Tunnel, the Redmires catch-water and land in the Ewden Valley, which was acquired to build Broomhead and Morehall Reservoirs. The latter were begun by the Corporation in 1913 but were not completed until 1929. The Waterworks Company's Parliamentary Act had also indicated the construction of reservoirs near Stocksbridge at Langsett and Underbank.

Problems inherited by the Corporation included things like the poisoning of local people from lead piping due to the acidity of water from Redmires, which came straight off the moorland bogs. The action taken was to lower the acidity by means of broken limestone at various places in the conduit and in the gauge basin of the reservoirs. Other issues arising were matters such as leakage due to poor construction. However, water supply was to enter a new era, as by the 1890s the Town Council had control and was now involved in disputes with other councils such as Rotherham, Barnsley and, for example, Dewsbury & Heckmondwike Water Works Board, who were all wanting to impound parts of the Little Don. Eventually a compromise was reached with support from Rotherham and Doncaster to include the supply to the former of 1.6 million gallons per day, and the latter for 1 million gallons per day. The Sheffield Corporation interest was able to supply its own citizens as well as selling supplies to other, smaller authorities. In 1919, the Corporation obtained powers to utilise the River Don (River Don Pumping Scheme) for compensation purposes and a plant was established at Wincobank for this.

By the time of the First World War, nationally there were 2,160 water undertakings, including 786 local authorities across the country. The Water Act of 1945 encouraged amalgamations of water companies and boards, and by 1963 the numbers had reduced to a hundred water boards, fifty local authorities and twenty-nine privately owned statutory water companies. In Sheffield and South Yorkshire, the Sheffield Corporation took over the water supply services of the urban districts of Mexborough and Wath and the rural districts of Rotherham and Kiveton Park in the 1960s (it had been supplying Rotherham and Doncaster since around 1900). The Water Act of 1973 fundamentally reorganised the water industry. It was removed from local authority control, and ten larger water authorities were set up. The Yorkshire Water Authority took over the functions of twenty-two local authorities across Yorkshire and parts of Derbyshire, including Sheffield City Council, Barnsley Borough Council, Rotherham Borough Council, the urban districts of Norton and Rawmarsh, the Doncaster and District Joint Water Board and the Yorkshire River Authority. In 1989 water authorities were privatised and the Yorkshire Water Authority became Yorkshire Water plc. Ten years later it became the largest subsidiary of Kelda Group plc.

Ultimately, through the twentieth century the Corporation Waterworks, despite many issues and problems, had evolved into the Water Board, Yorkshire Water Authority and then into Yorkshire Water plc, dealing with water supply and sewerage. By the later

1900s, water pollution control and associated statutory duties were separated off into the appropriate government body, which today is the Environment Agency. A major initiative during the 1960s and 1970s was the Sheffield Water Undertaking, which effectively adopted a grid-style approach to water supply by means of long-distance pipelines between supply catchments using pumping stations to hold water in larger reservoirs as needed. Similar schemes evolved elsewhere with cities like Manchester and Birmingham, for example, taking water from the heart of Wales or Cumbria to supply their needs. In 1899, the cities of Leicester and Derby sought powers to obtain rights over the headwaters of the River Derwent, above Bamford. Sheffield Corporation objected to this and instead agreement was reached in the formation of the Derwent Valley Water Board, constituted with members from Sheffield, Derby City, Leicester City, Nottingham City and Derbyshire County. The Board established reservoirs at Howden (1912), Derwent (1916) and Ladybower (1945), and via the Derwent Valley Water Works a pipeline was constructed to link this system to the Rivelin Reservoirs, about 5 miles to the east.

By the late 1960s, the Undertaking was supplying around 740,000 people across the Sheffield region with 227 million litres, or 50 million gallons, of water per day. The sources were a combination of the reservoirs already noted with water straight off the local moors, the Upper Derwent Valley Reservoirs of the Derwent Valley Water Board and a major long-distance supply from the Yorkshire Derwent at Elvington Water Treatment Station, near York. The last scheme was developed at a cost of £8 million as a fully automated project, with treatment works, pipelines, pumping stations and reservoirs to supply Sheffield, Barnsley, Leeds and Rotherham with about 68,000 cubic metres of water per day. Upgraded in the 1980s, the system became a critical part of the Yorkshire water grid, and supplied 182,000 cubic metres.

Forestry and Farming

Traditional rural industries are frequently overlooked when discussing the industrial history of Sheffield, and yet they are an intrinsic part of the story. In this consideration it is important firstly to separate 'woodlands' from 'forestry'. The former were managed sustainably to produce timber for construction and underwood, or wood, for fuelwood, charcoal and smaller construction. The latter was a system of management of plantations from the 1700s onwards to produce timber from mostly non-native trees such as conifers. Traditional woodland management essentially powered Sheffield's industrial revolution and the consequence of this is our almost unique heritage of 'ancient woodland' sites today. By the mid-1800s, almost all traditional woodland management was ending, and it ceased entirely by the 1950s.

Plantation forestry was a latecomer in landscape history terms, but with government grants following the formation of the Forestry Commission in 1919, it prospered in the areas around the urban fringe of Sheffield, particularly in the north and the west. Large areas of land were afforested by a variety of players, including the local authority, the larger private estates, the Forestry Commission itself and, of course, the water companies and undertakers in various guises. This grant-driven process continued well into the 1980s. Sheffield City Council plantations included Lady Canning's and Burbage Valley at Ringinglow, and in the Ewden Valley, while the water companies afforested areas around most of their reservoirs and the Forestry Commission developed large conifer stands at Wharncliffe Crags and around the Derwent Valley. Private forestry initiatives took place on most of the larger landed estates, for example the Fitzwilliam Estate plantations at Strines Moor, and other private initiatives (ultimately Fountain Forestry) at Grenoside. It was noted in the 1956 British Association volume *Sheffield and its Region* that:

> It has been the policy of the larger gravitational water authorities to plant trees on their gathering grounds especially in the immediate precincts of their reservoirs, the main purpose being the prevention of pollution from objectionable farming operations and the restriction of uncontrolled access by the public to the reservoirs and streams draining into the reservoirs. Growing trees, especially on steep slopes, are of considerable value in preventing soil erosion; they also tend to even out heavy rainfall and in due course provide valuable sources of pit props and other timber.

Timber is still harvested from these now mature plantations with some going to wood products and others to paper pulp and woodchip.

In terms of industrial development of Sheffield, farming is often entirely neglected. However, as the town grew to a city, and in the absence of refrigeration and rapid-transport systems, this expanding population needed feeding, and this was by local farms. Dairy products particularly were needed close at hand, and other foods too were locally sourced. Moreover, the early industry was powered by human labour and by animals, especially horses, and these needed oats and hay. So, as the industry expanded, the need for local farms also grew, and many of these were located almost in the heart of the city. The Manor Farm, which still functions today, though as a trust rather than a commercial enterprise, was perhaps the last of the truly urban farms to survive through the entire period. Ultimately, refrigeration, rail and then road transport, and the growth of nationally sourced supermarkets did for the rest.

Nevertheless, the Sheffield area has always had a busy agricultural industry around its suburbs with more intensive lowland farming to the south and east, and mixed upland and moorland farming (such as sheep) to the north and the west. Indeed, back in the 1980s, when I worked for Sheffield City Council, we had something like forty separate agricultural landholdings plus commercial forestry lands with a good number of tenant farmers and a farming and forestry team of around thirty people. This actually generated an annual income to the council of around £250,000 and my suggestion was to reinvest this income stream to draw down matching grant aid and to develop a genuinely sustainable approach to managing the city. However, due to central government financial and political pressures, the decision was taken to sell the 'family silver', and a one-off opportunity was missed. The capital re-sale value was of course nowhere near the long-term revenue that would have been due to the city and to the community. Many of the landholdings were acquired from the old Water Board when the Corporation relinquished its ownership of the water supply. Some of these upland-fringe assets were a modest cottage and a few fields so that Corporation water-workers could be paid only a part-time wage but they would be on hand when needed.

Another change in agriculture around the urban fringe has been the transition from commercial farming to 'horsey-culture' as recreational horse-riding has grown in popularity and as farms have been sold on for upmarket residential use. The other move since the 1960s has been the emergence of commercial horticulture and garden centres in the urban-fringe countryside; in some cases these developed from earlier market-gardening ventures that supplied the nearby townships. The other big change has of course been the transformation of countryside and farmed landscapes to urban industrial, commercial and residential uses.

Barker's Pool, Sheffield, in the 1700s.

A typical rural settlement with a group of cottages at The Green, Norton.

Former medieval ridge and furrow from the farming settlement at Norton. (Ian Rotherham)

Gathering raspberries at the
English Fruit Preserving Farm,
Stocksbridge, in August 1904.

A haystack at a farm
in Hemsworth, Norton.

Langsett Reservoir in the
1970s. (Ray Manley)

Underbank Reservoir
in the mid-1900s.

Rivelin Dams in
the 1950s.

Rivelin Dams from
Hollow Meadows in
the early 1900s.

Pine plantations at Wyming Brook Drive in the early 1900s.

Larch plantation at Wyming Brook Drive in the early 1900s.

West End Bridge and Howden Reservoir in the early 1900s.

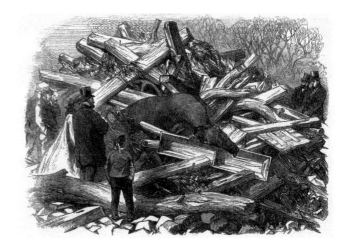

A scene in a garden at Hillsborough as a result of the Great Sheffield Flood, 1864.

Searching for the dead at Malin Bridge after the Great Sheffield Flood, 1864.

The Great Sheffield Flood, as seen from Langsett Road, 1864.

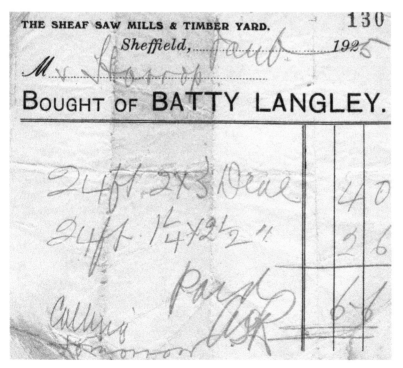

Above: Millhouses
Wood in
about 1906.

Left: Sheaf Saw
Mills & Timber
Yard sales ticket
from 1925.

Weir on River Don near Beeley Wood in the early 1900s.

Whiteley Woods in the early 1900s.

Other Manufacturing and Services

Glass-Making

The early origins of glass-making in and around Sheffield are poorly known. Glass was always a valuable material but in medieval times, or even before that, was an expensive luxury item. Nevertheless, by the 1600s at least there was a glass-making industry established in the area and particularly at Catcliffe in the south-east and at Bolsterstone in the north. In 1790, a glass manufacturer near Barnsley was making 'black glass bottles ... superior to any of the kind elsewhere'. At Bolsterstone, glass was manufactured by John Fox, who died in 1659, and the work continued with his nephew George Fox in the late 1600s. George's daughter married the works manager, William Fenney, and at this time the products from their works were of especially high quality, being 'carried to London and other places and sold at higher than market price by the name of London glass or some other name'. The works remained in the family during the 1700s, though they were inherited by Fenney's mother-in-law's son in 1757. It seems that this led to a degree of conflict over ownership but the mother-in-law's will also prevented Fenney from establishing his own glassworks within 10 miles of Bolsterstone. The result was that he transferred his operations and skills to the Catcliffe site, to where he was followed by the other Bolsterstone glassworkers. At Bolsterstone, glass production ended in 1778 and they converted to pottery manufacture. The glass-cones were built at Catcliffe in about 1740 and one still stands today, the oldest example of its sort in Europe. During the 1800s there were many other glass-works established across the South Yorkshire region, and at Catcliffe glass manufacture continued until the early 1900s.

Brewing

William Stones Ltd

Stones Brewery (William Stones Ltd) was a regional brewery founded in 1868 by William Stones in Sheffield, then in the Yorkshire West Riding. This became a well-established brew, with William Stones beginning his brewing operations in Sheffield in 1847 with

Joseph Watts. Then, following Watts' death in 1854, Stones continued alone, and in 1868 purchased the lease of the Neepsend Brewery. He renamed this the Cannon Brewery (the symbol of Stones Bitter) and continued brewing there until he died in 1894. The business was bought by Bass Brewery in 1968 and they subsequently closed down the Sheffield-based operation. Following closure in 1999, the headline brand 'Stones Bitter' [pronounced Stones-zz] was produced by Molson Coors Brewing Company, but even this ended in June 2012. As it turned out, this was a very bad decision commercially, since the beer's popularity grew to a peak in about 1992 as the country's best-selling bitter, with over 1 million barrels selling a year, and was described as 'one of Sheffield's most famous exports'.

However, Stones Bitter declined in popularity as the authenticity of the Sheffield production was lost. Apparently a member of the Bass board of directors involved in the closure decision later admitted that it was a bad misjudgement and especially so with a subsequent resurgence in taste for golden ales and local-provenance beer. Perhaps Bass should have backed Stones and not the southern brew, Worthington.

S. H. Ward & Co. Ltd

Wards Brewing Company was based at the Sheaf Brewery at the bottom of Ecclesall Road and ended up merely a subsidiary of Double Maxim Beer Company, with a bottled version of the beer being produced under licences at other sites. The most famous brand produced was Wards Best Bitter but they also produced a decent Ward's Mild too. Brewing had begun when, in 1837, William Roper and John Kiby set up on Effingham Street. However, Roper died in 1842 to leave John Kiby as the sole proprietor, until being joined by George Wright in 1860 and then by Septimus Henry Ward in 1868 as the business struggled. Because Ward financed the recovery of the brewery the main brand was renamed 'Wards Best Bitter', and George Wright left a year later. Wards now continued a policy of expansion and purchase of other breweries and their associated public houses. Finally, in 1876, they purchased the SOHO Brewery, which, renamed the Sheaf Brewery, became the main premises for S. H. Wards & Company Limited (established in 1896).

Wards carried on expanding during the early twentieth century through acquisition and renovation of licenced premises – a process that was slowed by lack of raw materials during the Second World War. During the 1940 Blitz, the brewery was struck by three incendiary bombs, resulting in the death of four workers. After the war ended, Wards recovered and began a further period of expansion.

Nevertheless, the end was on the horizon, and in 1972 Wards was taken over by Vaux & Associated Breweries, carrying on brewing bitter but as a subsidiary business. The Wards business remained a profitable brewery but was closed in 1999, when the Vaux interests were broken up following an aggressive takeover by financiers. The process was hugely controversial when, as members of the Vaux founding family, the Nicholsons, attempted a management buyout of the Sheaf Brewery the proposal was rejected. Following demolition of all but the most historic parts of the complex on site, the land was sold to developers to build luxury apartments and a bar. Unbelievably, and much to the chagrin of many locals, the price paid was several million pounds lower than the buyout offer and a big piece of local heritage was needlessly and, it seemed, maliciously destroyed. In 2003, the Wards marque was acquired by the Double Maxim Beer Company to be run by the Wards Brewing Company as a subsidiary. The bottled version was originally brewed and launched by Robinson's of Stockport, with a cask version (initially from Jennings of Cockermouth) also now from Robinsons and available in pubs. Branding still suggests, misleadingly, that Wards is from the Sheaf Brewery in Sheffield.

Tennant Brothers Ltd Sheffield

One of the famous local beers was that of Tennant Brothers Ltd Exchange Brewery on Bridge Street. Founded in 1820, the business was acquired by Tennant Brothers in 1840 until being taken over by Whitbread & Co. Ltd in 1961, and with 700 'tied houses' it became Whitbread East Pennines. The main brands brewed in Sheffield (450,000 barrels a year) were Trophy Bitter and Gold Label, famously strong ale sold in small bottles. As a student landscape gardener in the 1970s, I recall some of the men drinking this brew two bottles at a time, poured into a pint glass. However, closure followed in 1993, with the brew being transferred to Whitbread's five other breweries, and 186 local jobs were lost as a direct result. The iconic buildings remain at the site but have been mostly converted to offices.

Duncan Gilmour & Co. Ltd

Duncan Gilmour was born a Scot in 1816, and when sixteen years old moved to Ireland where he learnt the business of wines and spirits. By 1854, he had relocated to Sheffield and established Duncan Gilmour & Co., wine and spirit merchants, located at 56–58 Queen Street at premises called the Murrays Arms. Then, in 1860, Gilmour bought premises in Dixon Lane, where brewing began in 1884, and the venture was registered as a limited company in 1891. The founder had retired in 1883 and passed the business to a son, Duncan Gilmour Junior. Gilmour Senior died at Sandygate on 11 January 1889 and was buried at Christ Church, Fulwood. The company was bought by Joshua Tetley & Sons Ltd in 1954, though the brewery stayed open for some years after that. Over the years the brewery made a wide range of beers, stouts, pale ales, strong ales and more. At that time the business owned 148 licenced houses in Sheffield along with 350 premises and the Windsor Brewery in Liverpool. However, by 1964, Tetley had closed down the Sheffield brewing operation.

Contemporary Brewing

As the big breweries were taken over and then closed down by larger players during the later twentieth century, a quiet revolution was taking place. This was the emergence in the last twenty to thirty years of micro-breweries and craft breweries. The first was probably the Frog and Parrot pub on Division Street in the 1980s, brewing a rather lethal beer called 'Roger and Out'. A key point in the revolution, however, was the 1990s establishment of the Kelham Island Brewery, based out of the Fat Cat on Alma Street. Others were to follow with the Abbeydale Brewery, The Bradfield Brewery, and not actually in Sheffield but owning a number of Sheffield pubs, the Thornbridge Brewery of Bakewell. What goes around comes around and there are already rumours of the bigger players sniffing around the successful new enterprises.

Sheffield's Short-Lived Motor Industry

One of the forgotten facets of Sheffield is the short-lived motor manufacturing industry. Surprisingly from a twenty-first century perspective, there were quite a few engineering entrepreneurs willing to have a go, and some were actually pretty good. The following were some of the bigger names:

- Hallamshire: Durham Churchill & Co., Chambers Lane, Brightside, Sheffield, in production from 1901 to 1906.
- Cavendish: Sheffield Motor Company, Cavendish Street, Sheffield, in production from 1903 to 1905.
- La Plata: Burgon & Ball Ltd, Malin Bridge, Sheffield, but it is believed that most of their cars were 'badged' versions from other manufacturers.
- Sheffield-Simplex: Sheffield-Simplex Motor Works Ltd, Tinsley, Sheffield, in production from 1906 to 1922.
- YEC: The Yorkshire Engine Co., Sheffield, production dates unknown.
- Stringer: Stringer & Company (Sheffield) Ltd, Wincobank Steel Works, Sheffield, in production from 1913 to around 1932.
- Richardson: C. E. Richardson & Co. Ltd, Finbat Works, Aizlewood Road, Sheffield, in production from 1919 to 1921.
- HFG: C. Portass & Son, Broadfield Rd, Sheffield, in production from around 1919 to 1921.
- Charron Laycock: W. S. Laycock Ltd, Archer Road, Millhouses, Sheffield, in production from 1919 to about 1927.

The Simplex and the Richardson were the stand-out brands and the former was regarded by many as the best motor of its time. There is now a 1921 C. E. Richardson & Co. vehicle, registration number U 9296, on exhibition at Kelham Island Industrial Museum. Charles Ebenezer Richardson and Ernest Richardson were the sons of Ebenezer Richardson and had started up in motor manufacture from the modest beginnings of making children's scooters. However, from 1919 to 1922 from their Finbat Works on Aizlewood Road in Sheffield they produced around 600 cars with the staggering horsepower of 8 hp and 10 hp. A smart-looking, lightweight car seating two and weighing 7 cwt, the Richardson was designed by Albert Clarke and was exhibited at the Olympia Motor Car Show and at White City, London.

Sheffield's Rolls-Royce, however, was the Sheffield-Simplex of Sheffield and Kingston upon Thames, also known as Sheffield-Simplex Motor Works. The Sheffield factory was situated by the junction of Lock Lane and Sheffield Road and was just west of Templeborough Rolling Mills. The factory was connected to the Great Central Railway's Sheffield & Mexborough Branch, located north of the premises. The Simplex received financial backing from the regional coal magnate and Sheffield industrialist Earl Fitzwilliam. He had been an investor in a car called the Brotherhood-Crocker, which was made in London. However, Brotherhood had sold the London site in 1905 and moved to Peterborough, but once there had failed to get planning consent for his new premises. Earl Fitzwilliam, one of Brotherhood's investors, suggested a move to Sheffield, whereupon he built the new factory in Tinsley. There was clear logic in relocating to a city famous for its steel and for its precision engineering skills. The first few cars were called Brotherhoods as a continuation of the cars originally made in London. In 1905, they produced three sizes of car (in length) but each with the same 20 hp, four-cylinder engine and chain-driven. At the 1906 Olympia Exhibition, the Sheffield-Simplex and the Brotherhood were presented together on the same stand, but in late 1906 Peter Brotherhood withdrew from the car venture. Then, in 1908, the first cars to just bear the Sheffield-Simplex name appeared, designed by Percy Richardson, who was ex-Daimler and Brotherhood. The LA1 had a six-cylinder 6,978cc engine and three-speed gearboxes; in 1908, there was also the LA2 intended for lighter, open bodies, without a conventional gear system. By 1909, they were thinking of building engines for aeroplanes, worked on designs and even bought a Blériot monoplane.

Further models were produced in 1910, and by 1911 these were replaced by the LA7 with a six-cylinder, 4,740cc engine. This meant they could boast that only one other British car-maker made only six-cylinder cars, with the Sheffield-Simplex company considering their only rival to be Rolls-Royce. By 1913 they even included electric starting and in 1925 introduced a dipping headlamp system.

During the First World War the Sheffield-Simplex company made armoured cars, which were supplied to the Belgian and Russian armies. They also made ABC Wasp and Dragonfly aircraft engines and munitions. Motor car production recommenced in 1919 and new models were on show in London in 1920 and in 1921. However, sales were not good and the company branched out in 1923 to build the 'Ner-A-Car' motorcycle from a factory in Kingston upon Thames. This was a rather unconventional motorbike designed by American Carl Neracher with a very low chassis slung down between the wheels and was in production for just four years.

The last years of Sheffield-Simplex company car production are unclear but few were sold after the end of the war, and those may have been from the London factory. Overall, they made around 1,500 cars but almost none remain. In the 1960s and 1970s, Lord Riverdale, having acquired the one-time Sheffield-Simplex factory in Sheffield, set about rebuilding one from parts that came from far-flung places like Australia! I have been told that he used to drive it at speed around the Peak District. Still in private ownership, the vehicle remains in use and appears at shows in Derbyshire and Yorkshire. It is suggested that three cars have survived, including a unique 50 hp vehicle produced and exhibited in 1920. This was acquired by Earl Fitzwilliam in 1925 after the liquidation of the Sheffield business and today is in Kelham Island Museum. There are also the ex-Lord Riverdale car (which he drove from Land's End to John o' Groats without changing from top gear) and one at the Powerhouse Museum, Sydney, Australia.

Overall, as Sheffield grew from a parochial border settlement on the River Don to a small medieval town, and ultimately to a world-leading industrial city, it acquired and developed all the trades, industries and crafts associated with such a place. Initially, of course, most raw materials and the bulk of products had to be extracted, grown, harvested and manufactured in the locale. With transport very difficult, long-distance trade was limited, and mostly comprised essential materials unavailable locally, or luxury goods. Nearby towns like Barnsley, for example, had an almost forgotten fame as a linen-producing centre, and Sheffield boasted a cotton mill on the Rover Don. Another industry that evolved on a modest scale from medieval times, but grew significantly into the industrial period, was tanning. This was an industry linked closely to the ancient oak woods of the area since the tanyards and tanners require a good supply of oak-bark provided by 'barkers' working the woods. Around Sheffield, Handsworth and Woodhouse were notable centres, and Chesterfield was a famously smelly tanning town! Other important commercial enterprises that flourished for a good while were things like snuff manufacture and the famous Wilson's snuff mill at Sharrow.

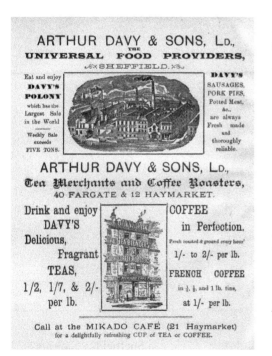

Above left: Advert for Arthur Davy & Sons, food providers, from 1896.

Above right: Cast-iron stoves from Moorwoods of Harleston Street in the 1930s.

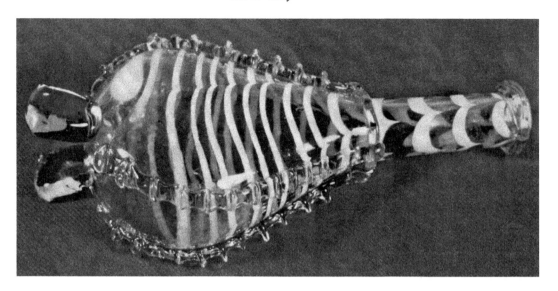

Above: Catcliffe glass flask.

Left: Catcliffe Glassworks.

Established 1866.   Tel. No.: Central 2368.

JOHN SCHOLEY & SONS
(F. W. SCHOLEY, Proprietor)
56 Garden Street, SHEFFIELD.

MANUFACTURERS OF
STEEL STAMPS, LETTERS,
FIGURES, MARKS,
BRANDS, &c.
ON H.M. WAR OFFICE AND OTHER LISTS.

[2]

Above: John Scholey & Sons of Garden Street, manufacturers of steel stamps in the 1930s.

Right: Pikelet shop baker on Devonshire Street in the early 1900s.

The 1913
Sheffield-Simplex
landaulette with
coachwork
by Pytchley.

Wilson's Snuff
Mill at Sharrow in
the 1970s.

Stokes & Co.,
manufacturer of
paints, varnishes
and enamels in
the 1930s.

Above left: Wilson's snuff.

Above right: The Sheffield-Simplex – 'Your car is the finest I have ever driven' and is '... unapproached as a triumph of engineering'.

Below: The Ivory Room at the works of Messrs Rodgers & Sons, 1800s.

The Impacts on People

Sheffield's rise to industrial success and fame was due to location, water power and access to minerals and other resources, but also because of its growing tradition for skilled craftsmanship. It was upon the reputation for fine craftsmanship that Sheffield's industry grew. Furthermore, as metal manufacture and then processing of metals into high-quality products developed, so did the specialist skills – the hand raiser, the piercer, the chaser, the engraver, the burnisher and more. As the city's reputation grew, Sheffield attracted more business and more people to train and work in the emerging industries, and so a dramatic population rise followed the industrialisation. Indeed, from around 1800 to 1850, the town expanded from a population of 31,000 to 135,000, of whom around a third were inward migrants. However, with much of the available space increasingly filled by workshops, what remained for housing was limited, and this resulted in mass 'back-to-back' houses and a growing squalor. Jerry-built, the properties were three-storey terraces but joined by the back wall, with one house on the back and one on the front, each with a single lower room and another above. These homes were generally centred on a shared yard with up to twenty families sharing a single drain and a tap or water-pump, which operated for perhaps two hours per day just three days per week. An example of the atrocious conditions can be seen in the 150-yard-long Bailey Street with forty workshops and 192 houses, which housed 800 people. The streets were cleaned to some degree but the courtyards were not and so they accumulated a festering mix of ashes, slops, excrement and other waste. With cesspits, shared latrines and ground-water pumps, the setting was ripe for catastrophic outbreaks of disease. In 1832, an epidemic of cholera broke out and surprisingly killed just 402 people; it could have been much worse. Nevertheless, this was a warning to the authorities, who began to take or at least plan actions to improve living conditions.

However, the expansion continued as Sheffield's industrial prowess and reputation grew, and more people were sucked in to the crowded town, the population of the now city increased further, hitting 380,000 by 1900. As the city sprawled outwards it subsumed and absorbed surrounding villages and settlements such as Heeley, Walkley, Attercliffe, Crookes, Hillsborough, Handsworth and Woodhouse. By 1864 there were around 19,000 back-to-backs, but in 1892 the council began the slow process of slum clearance. Additionally, as the Corporation took over responsibility for water supply in 1888, the intention was to provide every dwelling with running water. Drainage and sanitation remained major problems though, with open or rubble sewers becoming blocked, complicating their inherently unhygienic design. These began to be replaced by sealed pipes in the 1890s and water-closets replaced ash-pits and privy middens.

Across the wider region, rural communities began a rapid transformation and de-population. The poorer people and the less affluent peasants, who formerly subsisted in the countryside, became rural, often seasonal labour, or were unemployed. Many migrated to the cities and towns that in turn spread out across the once green landscapes. Growth was a mix of increased birth rates and inward migration. Though material conditions like housing were better in the town than the countryside, the situation rapidly deteriorated, with services and provisions becoming overwhelmed. By the 1800s, the land, air and water were grossly polluted, and mortality in the urban centres grew alarmingly. Factories and houses now burnt raw coal (tens of thousands of tons per year) and the smoke was deadly. Air pollution took its toll in bronchial diseases exacerbated by exposure to metallic waste and dust inhaled in the cramped confined spaces of urban industrial sweatshops. By the 1970s, Sheffield University Medical School was the place to study if you wanted to gain experience in nasty industrial diseases from metalworking or mining, or in serious industrial accidents.

Along with air pollution, as noted earlier, the town's water supplies were a source of disease and death as cholera and typhoid took their toll. So, in the mid-1800s, the mean life expectancy in inner city Sheffield was around twenty years, and by 1843 the average age of people dying in the city centre was just twenty-four years. In 1866, the local rivers were described as 'conduits of all imaginable filth ... polluted with dirt, dung, dust and carrion ... overhung with privies', and the people were noted as being 'compelled to breathe so large an amount of putrefying refuse'. With chronically poor public health and acute industrial diseases, the brand 'Made in Sheffield' came at a cost in human life and suffering.

Sheffield and its region were a powerhouse not only for England, but also for the world beyond. As the British Empire spread around the planet, materials manufactured and produced here spread as a global brand. This reached a peak in the mid-twentieth century as a slow decline began in the aftermath of the Second World War. However, the emerging city was not just an industrial centre, and as an economic hub it drew in and nurtured academics and philosophers, writers, artists, industrialists, inventors and politicians. From the energy of industry grew an engine of social and educational development and reform. Yet this emergence was in the face of a rapid decline in social welfare, in health and in quality of life for the vast majority of people. The other major cost was in the almost total decline in environmental quality as rivers once rich in salmon and other fish became dead, stinking sewers, while riverside pastures and meadows were destroyed or grossly polluted.

In closing this chapter, which reminds us of the cost of industrial progress – paid by people and nature – it is worth mentioning some hazards and diseases peculiar or at least especially prevalent in Sheffield. The 'little mesters' and their workers toiled in confined and enclosed spaces; if one of the huge grindstones broke then the consequences were disastrous. The stones might 'burst' as they revolved and in the scythe- and saw-grinding trades these beasts, 6 feet in diameter, weighed in at around 2 tons apiece. If they did break into pieces anyone in the working space would be killed or maimed. However, it was the small stuff that really killed insidiously, with tiny particles of sandstone and steel or other metals pervading the atmosphere and being inhaled. The most well-known version of this was Grinder's Disease:

> Their complexions assume a dirty, muddy appearance ... they complain of tightness across the chest, the voice is rough and hoarse, their cough loud ... Diarrhoea, extreme emaciation, together with all the usual symptoms of pulmonary consumption at length carries them off, but not until they have lingered through months and even years of suffering, incapable of working to support themselves or their families.

There were other variants that killed at least as effectively. Dust might be reduced by 'wet grinding' with water but many workers continued with 'dry grinding' and there was no dust-extraction system, meaning that few lived beyond thirty years.

By the nineteenth century, with minimal education a boy of eight years would be working with his father. In order to become a craftsman, a formal seven-year apprenticeship would begin at around thirteen years of age with good instruction or poor from a master who paid very little. The work that then followed would be for around a seventy-hour week with twelve-hour shifts, for example in the rolling mills or forges. Holidays were few and far between and wages were low – perhaps £3 a week as a top wage for skilled grinders or steel melters, for example, and most others earned much lower. There were few leisurely recreations in the mid-1800s, other than drink and associated diversions, with 1 per cent of the population being charged with public drunkenness in 1851. Other pursuits and education were even frowned upon as they might give rise to unrest, trade unionism and a tendency to speechmaking. The craftsman often worked until he died prematurely or else was so badly invalided that, unable to work on, he fell upon the poorhouse or workhouse to be fed and clothed by charity until death took him away.

In considering Sheffield's industries, it has been necessary to move quickly over a wide range of topics and to omit some completely. For example, the city was hugely important in both military and naval armour plate, and in munitions; each of these might otherwise merit a chapter. The now famous Sheffield Buffer Girls would be another such story to merit a chapter. The Buffer Girls worked in the metal industries and were responsible for polishing cutlery, silverware and other metal goods to give them a smooth surface. The work was hard and very dirty, so neckerchiefs and headscarves were worn to help keep clean. In the early 1900s, they were paid about 5s a week. The Buffer Girls were especially important during the wartime effort when male labour was in short supply, and many women worked in munitions.

Chatting to Mac Jackson of Totley, he came up with a personal account of one such industrial workshop largely lost from memory – the Naval Ordnance Inspection Establishment (NOIE). This was Sheffield's own official 'naval dockyard', and also named HMS *Scylla*. On site was the Bragg Laboratory, a metallurgy research facility. The site was on Janson Street, Attercliffe Common, between Janson Street, Amberly Street, Bold Street and Cardiff Street. NOIE was an Admiralty-run gauge factory employing over 150 engineers and admin staff to make gauges specifically for the Navy. These measured the size of a box or a shell, or helped alignment of fins on missiles. This is just one example of a forgotten past.

Today's Industries and the Future

From the 1970s into the 1990s, the city and region entered a rapid and dramatic downturn in their industrial base. Furthermore, while a reorganised specialist steel sector continued to thrive, it now employed relatively small numbers of people. At the start of the 1970s, the industrial Lower Don Valley in Sheffield employed around 70,000 people directly and many more in related service industries. Most of these people lived in tightly packed communities in and around the valley where they worked. Almost overnight, the jobs and the people had gone for ever.

This was a time of economic decline, of identity crisis for the city and its communities, of unemployment and strikes, of energy shortages and the 1970s 'Three-Day Week', of the 1980s and Margaret Thatcher, the North-South divide and political crisis and unrest. Miners took to the streets in protest and were brutally suppressed by police brought in from London. Coalmines closed, factories closed, land lay derelict and entire communities were out of work. Where large factories remained, they were increasingly vulnerable to being taken over by capitalists from elsewhere, outside the city or even outside the UK. When this happens, local people lose what control they might have had in determining their own destinies.

There were also major regional issues of competition for investment and for jobs and status with competition between Sheffield with Leeds to the north, Nottingham to the south and Manchester to the west. This remains a deeply divisive issue for people and for politicians.

In the 1950s, fuelled in part by a realisation and indeed the embarrassment of mass deaths due to air pollution – i.e. smog from industrial and domestic coal-burning – Sheffield pioneered the idea of Clean Air and Smokeless Zones. Combined with laws to protect watercourses from pollution and to control land degradation too, this began a slow process of urban ecological renewal. Ironically, the changes were speeded up by the closure of many of the factories that had been responsible for the problems. However, Sheffield, once famed as the Dirty City in a Golden Frame, began to grow a sense of civic pride as the Clean Air City, and by the 1980s, as a Green City.

From these beginnings in the 1980s there developed an interest in the potential for a genuine renewal of the landscape and ecology of the Lower Don Valley, the city's former industrial heartland. Indeed, with little prospect of economic renewal, the derelict and despoiled landscape was seen as a barrier to investment. Furthermore, even without intervention, nature was quickly reclaiming miles of unused former factory sites. However, in planning and political terms, the idea of greening the Don Valley was a precursor or even a trigger and catalyst for economic renewal, which gained support. Grants were available to remove pollution and to regenerate the landscape with massed tree and shrub planting, and the creation of new public open spaces and wildlife reserves. Access began by opening up riversides and canals for people to walk along and to provide much-improved footpaths and other facilities. Much of this work was led by local people determined to take action to improve their future. A planning and landscape vision for the Lower Don Valley was developed by the City Council and then by the short-lived Sheffield Development Corporation (SDC). A fast-track planning process and available finance, both administered by the SDC, provided catalysts for investment, renewal and redevelopment, and Sheffield began to turn a critical corner in its emergence as a modern city. Transformation from industrial to post-industrial was now well underway.

Central to the emergence of Sheffield as a modern and truly European city were a number of concepts and ideas that challenged the very roots of the industrial city's identity. The first of these was the intention to 'green' the former industrial areas and so to change perceptions about them and their possible futures. The second idea, which was even more controversial, was to build Europe's largest shopping centre at Meadowhall, on former industrial land. This was central to the then new concept of leisure shopping. The idea was to merge retail and leisure with food and entertainment. The third component was to brand Sheffield as the UK Sports City and to trigger this by hosting the relatively unknown World Student Games in 1991. This resulted in a massive commitment to capital investment in infrastructure, a transformation of greenspace, a total renewal of transport provision to link the city centre to peripheral regions and to thread together the sporting, leisure and retail facilities by new arterial roads and buses, by cycleways and walkways, and by a new high-tech electric Supertram. Sheffield was to become a city of sport, of shopping and leisure, and of tourism. For many local people, this seemed more than a little far-fetched.

These steps were hugely controversial and received little political support from the national government at Westminster. This meant that a consequence for Sheffield was that, in order to proceed, the City Council plunged itself and its community into a long-term debt that only now is close to being repaid. The step was a big gamble since it depended utterly on the combined success of all these actions and interventions. The political fallout was considerable and there were casualties in the City Council. Twenty-five years on, the gamble has paid off and the vision has become a reality, which is even more remarkable when the lack of central government support is considered. However, on the back of regional economic planning and forceful negotiating, the region did gain two major external funding streams, both from Europe. One was the Coalfields Development Fund, for former coal mining areas, and the other was Objective 1 status for South Yorkshire. These two financial mechanisms enabled many of the necessary infrastructure transformations to happen, without which the other economic renewals would not have taken place. Emerging in the post-industrial era, there have been a number of key economic forces:

• Retail and leisure
• Leisure and entertainment

- Sport and events
- Tourism – including industrial museums (the first in the world) and the Peak National Park (the first in Britain)
- High-tech and service industries
- Education – with two major universities and 50,000 students
- Health provision and hospitals
- Local authority and local service provision

A major controversy and a problem for regional regeneration was the tension between the Lower Don Valley and the old city centre. This was especially the case for the established city centre shops, which, failing to compete with the allure of Meadowhall, went into steep decline. This was always going to be the case and there were other deeply ingrained problems with the city centre's layout and facilities, even without the new competition. However, in the 1990s, a concept emerged called the 'Heart of the City Project' grew to provide a vision and plan for renewal of the urban centre. Again this has included new faculties, carefully designed public spaces and greenery, spectacular artwork and a reorganised and improved transport system. This has been hugely successful and its final stages were recently completed, while the regeneration of the Moor, of Shalemoor and West Bar, and of Charter Row are still ongoing. The city centre is now a transformed and vibrant area with plazas and piazzas, fountains and avenues, street cafés, museums, theatres and galleries. The modern city has a genuinely European feel about it, and is popular with locals and visitors alike. With leisure day-visitors and tourists, and especially international visitors because of the two universities, Sheffield is truly a city transformed.

The severe negative impacts of Meadowhall on other regional shopping and social loci such as Rotherham town centre have yet to be successfully resolved, but the city centre has responded and change is afoot. Indeed, the economic renewal and the transformation of former dereliction of heavy industry have rejuvenated much of Sheffield. City-centre living has also come back into vogue with upmarket apartments and student accommodation occupying former factories, workshops and warehouses, and also purpose-built new premises.

Much of the new economic activity is around high-tech business and also education. The two universities, with over 50,000 students between them, employ thousands of people directly and many more indirectly through service provision, retail, leisure and more. One of the more recent outcomes from university/private sector collaboration has been the development on former industrial land of the Advanced Manufacturing Park, or AMP, mixing high-tech research with heavy engineering skills. However, the manufacture of specialist steels is still huge in the city and Sheffield is still a world leader. The globally renowned cutlery and knife-manufacturing industries have struggled against cheap copies and poor-quality mass-production, but are still there, with Sheffield industry often bouncing back after downturns.

There remain controversies, such as the HS2, which is environmentally damaging at many levels but from which, with little hard evidence, is promised an economic miracle. Upgrading and electrification of existing routes could bring most of the benefits at a fraction of the social, environmental and economic costs. From the perspective of Sheffield's industry the key questions are probably to do with the ability to capitalise on these major infrastructural projects and to be the region that delivers. The wind farm revolution is one example, where in the past Sheffield might have led the way in designing and manufacturing the units, but for various reasons this wasn't the case. Hopefully, the presence of the AMP and the two major universities will help ensure that future opportunities do not go begging.

Finally, in contrast to our history of heavy and often dirty industry, Sheffield has a growing reputation as a destination for outdoor activities (the City of the Great Outdoors), for retail leisure, for sport, leisure and entertainment, for cultural industries and for tourism. Along with traditional industries and services, these are now the powerful economic drivers for a greener and more pleasant city of the twenty-first century, yet one with proud, rich and diverse industrial heritage.

Above left: The Sheffield University Arts Tower. (Ian Rotherham)

Above right: The Owen Building at Sheffield Hallam University. (Ian Rotherham)

Above left: Don Valley Stadium in the 1990s.

Above right: One of the last 'little mesters' – Peter Gribben at Abbeydale Industrial Hamlet. (Ian Rotherham)

Below: Abbeydale Industrial Hamlet is now a museum. (Ian Rotherham)

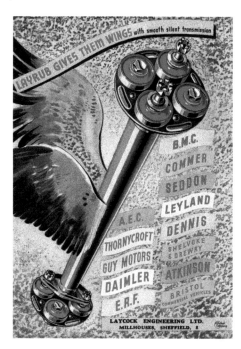

Above left: Laycock Engineering at Millhouses, Sheffield, in 1954, and a precursor of Sheffield's reputation for advanced engineering.

Above right: Laycock Engineering at Millhouses, Sheffield, in 1956.

Below: The Crucible. (Ian Rotherham)

Right: Meadowhall Shopping Centre. (Ian Rotherham)

Below: Western Bank and Sheffield University in the early 1900s.

WESTERN BANK AND UNIVERSITY, SHEFFIELD.

A flight from the short-lived Sheffield Airport at Tinsley in the 1990s.

The Lyceum. (Ian Rotherham)

The Sheffield Royal Grammar School and Collegiate in the early 1900s.

Bibliography

Barraclough, K. C. (1976) *Sheffield Steel* (Ashbourne: Moorland Publishing).

Davey, S. R. (undated) *'Where t'watter runs o'er t'weir': A Look Back at Sheffield's Watermills* (Sheffield: Parker Press Ltd).

Farnsworth, K. (1987) *Sheffielder's East Enders: Life as it was in the Lower Don Valley* (Sheffield: Sheffield City Libraries).

Hawson, H. K. (1968) *Sheffield: The Growth of a City 1893–1926* (Sheffield: J. W. Northend Ltd).

Hey, D. (1979) *The Making of South Yorkshire* (Ashbourne: Moorland Publishing).

Hey, D. (1991) *The Fiery Blades of Hallamshire: Sheffield and its Neighbourhood 1660–1740* (Leicester: Leicester University Press).

Hey, D. (1998) *A History of Sheffield* (Lancaster: Carnegie Publishing Ltd).

Hey, D. (2002) *Historic Hallamshire: History in Sheffield's Countryside* (Ashbourne: Landmark Publishing).

Hunter, J. (1869 edition) *The History and Topography of the Parish of Sheffield: With Historical and Descriptive Notices of the Parishes of Ecclesfield, Hansworth, Treeton and Whiston, and of the Chapelry of Bradfield* (Sheffield: Pawson & Brailsford).

Jones, M. (2000) *The Making of the South Yorkshire Landscape* (Barnsley: Wharncliffe Books).

Jones, M. (2003) *South Yorkshire Yesterday: Glimpses of the Past* (Skipton: Smith Settle).

Lewis, G. D. (1964) *The South Yorkshire Glass Industry* (Sheffield: Sheffield City Museum).

Linton, D. L. (ed.) (1956) *Sheffield and its Region: A Scientific and Historical Survey* (Sheffield: British Association, Local Executive Committee).

Oldham, D. C. (2010) *A History of Rolled Heavy Armour Plate Manufacture at the Sheffield Works of Charles Cammell and Vickers* (Sheffield: South Yorkshire Industrial History Society).

Rotherham, I. D. (2015) *Lost Sheffield in Colour.* (Stroud: Amberley Publishing).

Rotherham, I. D. (2017) *The Industrial Transformation of South Yorkshire Landscapes.*

Rotherham, I. D. & Handley, C. (eds) (2017) *The Industrial Legacy & Landscapes of Sheffield and South Yorkshire* (Sheffield: Wildtrack Publishing).

Smithurst, P. (1983) *A Guide to Sheffield's Industrial History* (Sheffield: Sheffield City Museum).

Walton, M. (1948) *Sheffield: Its Story and its Achievements* (Sheffield: The Sheffield Telegraph & Star Limited).

Warman, C. R. (1969) *Sheffield Emerging City* (Sheffield: City of Sheffield Town Planning Committee).

Acknowledgments

Many people have helped over the years with observations, information, and inspiration. The Sheffield Industrial Museums Trust and Peter Gribben are thanked for access to Abbeydale Industrial Hamlet. The countless photographers and artists who have left us a legacy of pictures of the city's industrial heritage over the centuries can't be thanked individually, and indeed many are today unknown, but I am grateful to them all. All images, unless otherwise credited, are from the personal collection of the author. The editorial and production team at Amberley are thanked for their help and especially their patience.

About the Author

Ian Rotherham is Professor of Environmental Geography and Reader in Tourism & Environmental Change at Sheffield Hallam University. He is an environmental historian and a worldwide authority on ecology, landscape history and on tourism and leisure. Born in Sheffield, Ian established and directed Sheffield City Council's Ecology Service within the City Museums Department, writes for the *Sheffield Star*, *Sheffield Telegraph* and the *Yorkshire Post* newspapers, and has a regular phone-in on BBC Radio Sheffield. He is a regional ambassador for Sheffield and the region and has written, edited and published over 400 papers, articles, books and book chapters. He lectures widely to local groups and works closely with conservation organisations and agencies. His recent books include *Lost Sheffield in Colour*, *Secret Sheffield*, *Sheffield Pubs*, *Sheffield in 50 Buildings* and several others for Amberley Publishing.